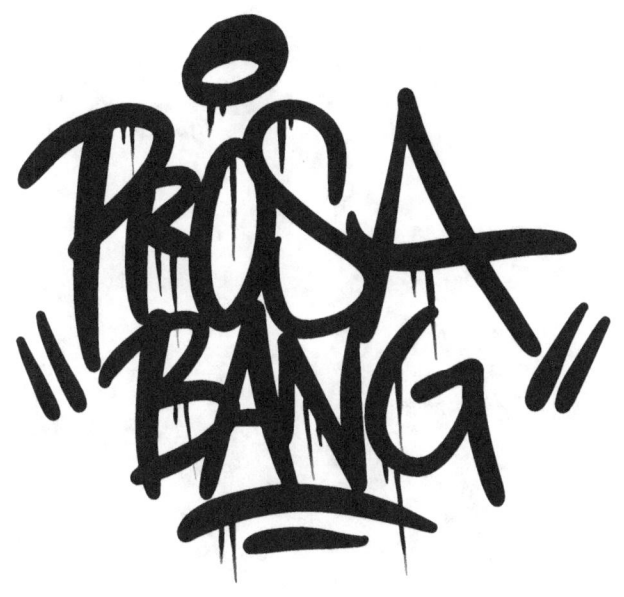

Copyright ©2020 by Simon Editions. All rights reserved.
No part of this book may be reproduced in any form and in any media, without written permission from the author, except for the use of brief quotation in reviews.
All third party trademarks (including logos) remain the property of their respective owners.

Please leave a review on Amazon if you enjoy it.

Hi! Do you remember me?
Did you enjoy coloring food with sneakers?
Are your markers ready for a new challenge?
In this book Mr.Bang is playing sports.
What are you waiting for?
Grab your marker and start to color!
I can't wait to see your works!

Enjoy!

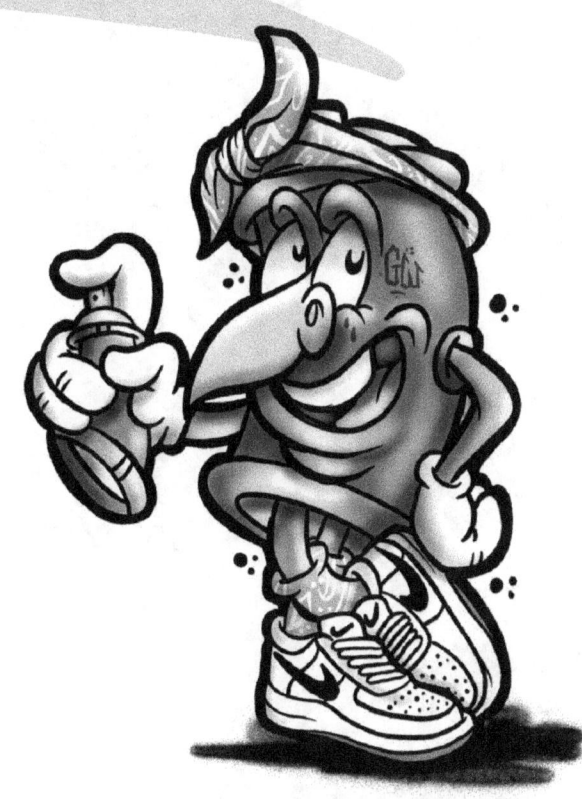

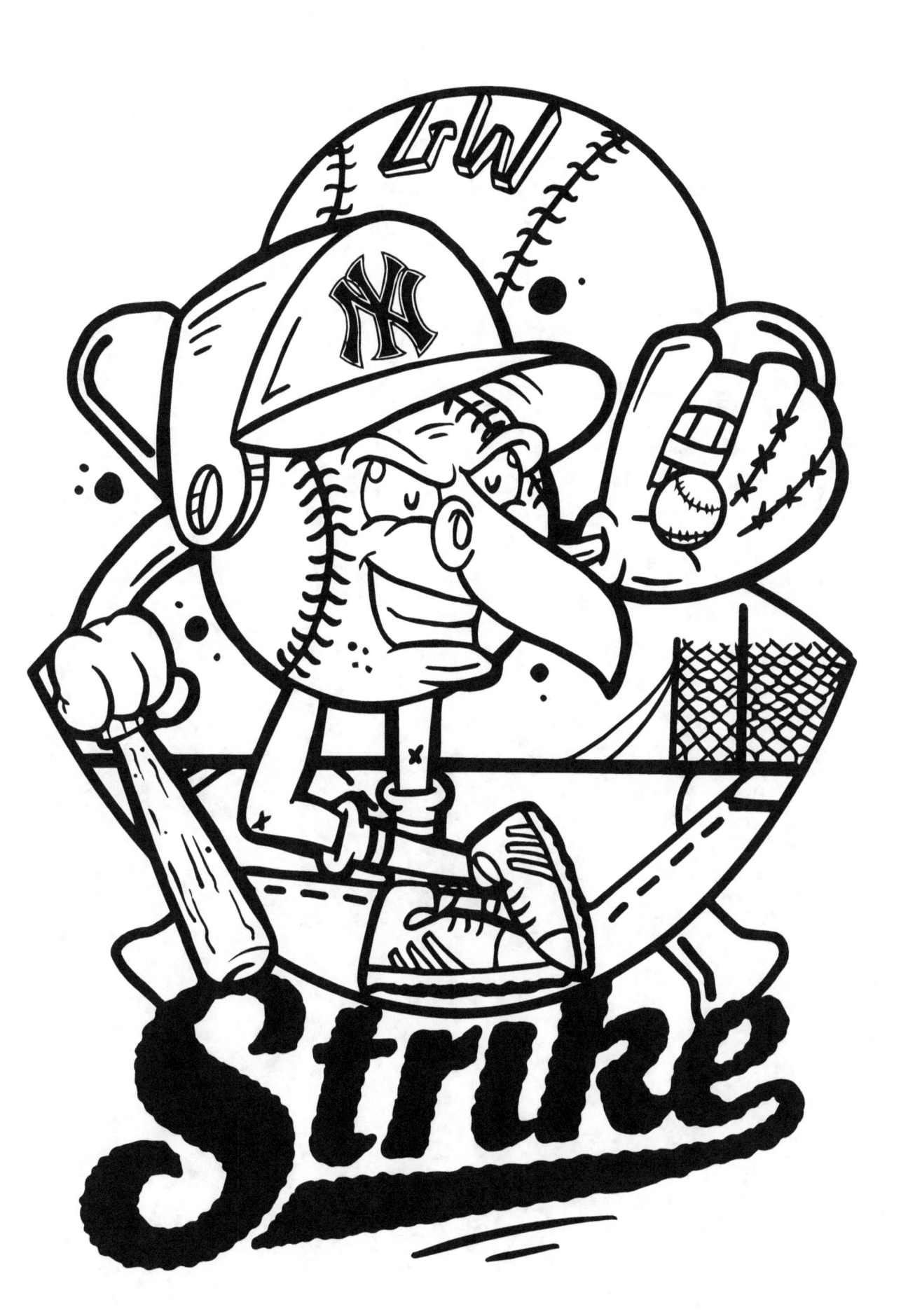

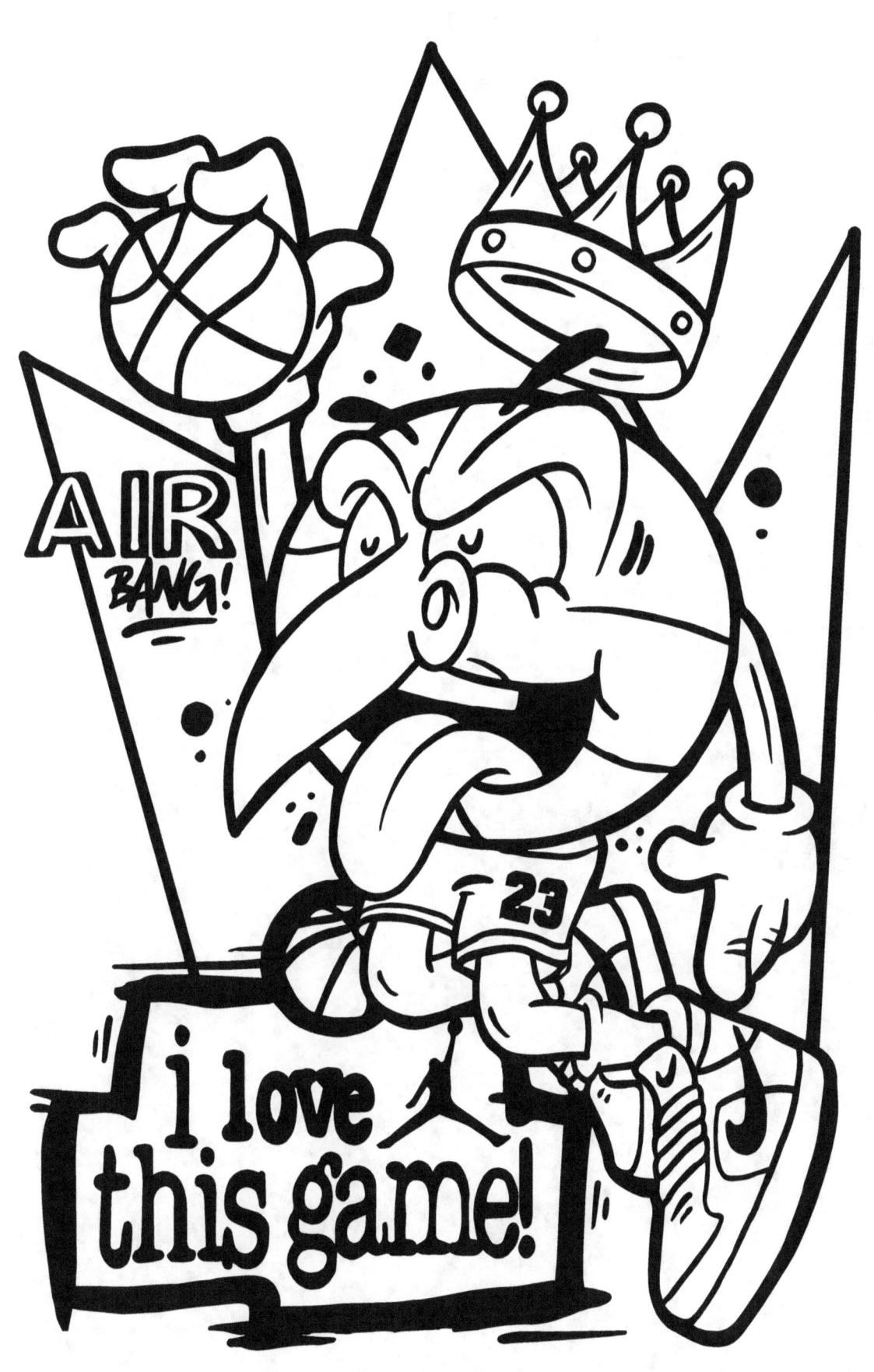

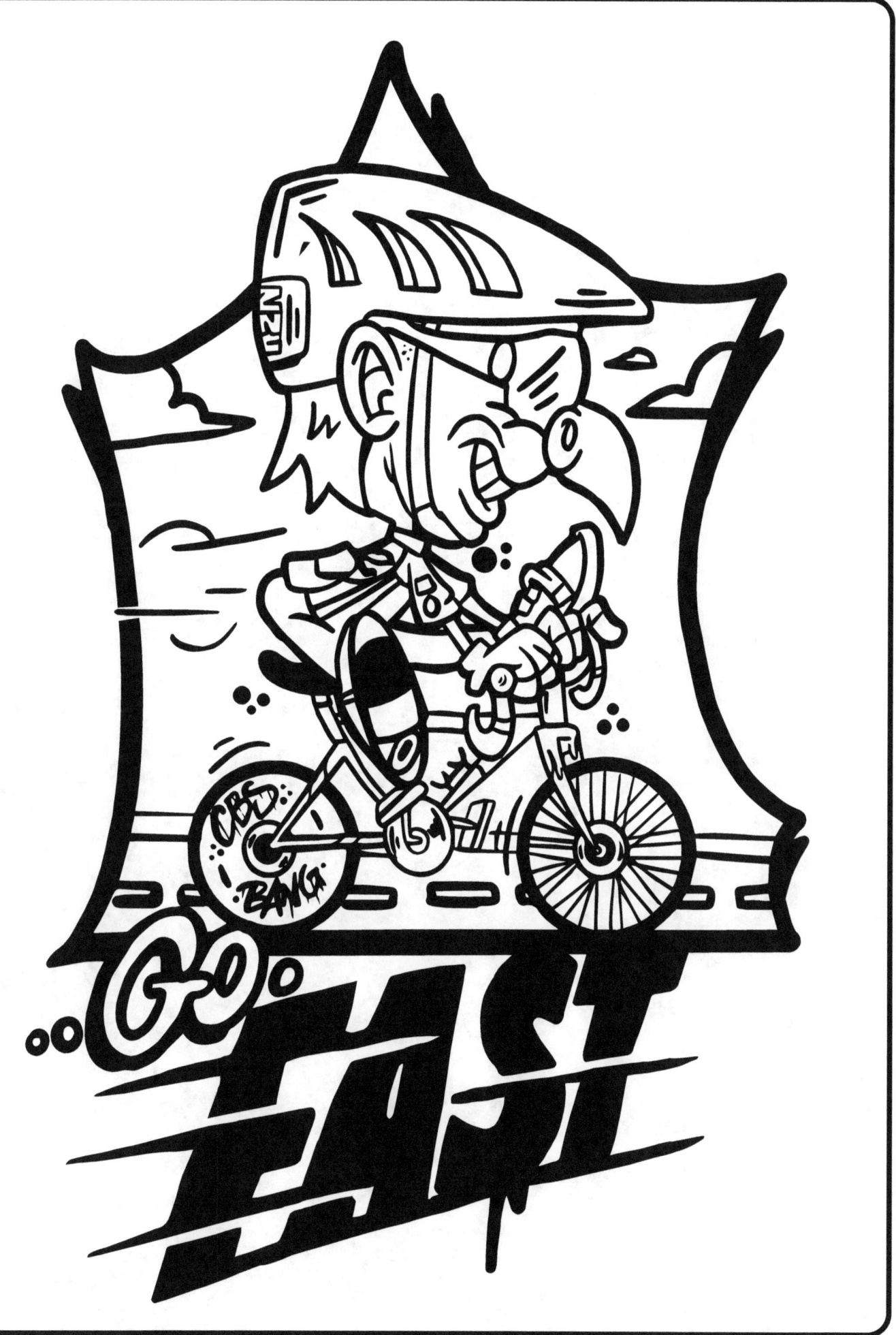

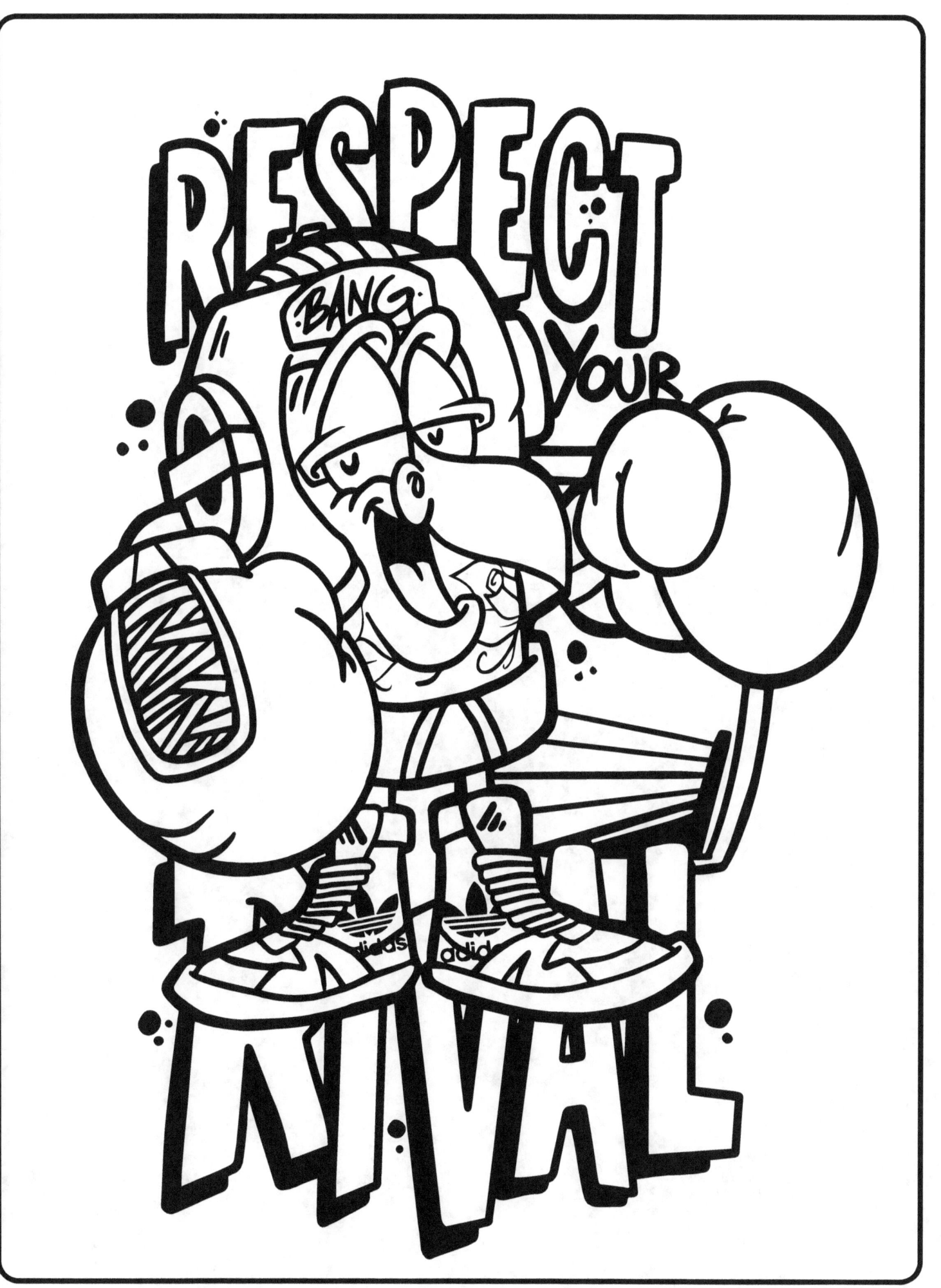

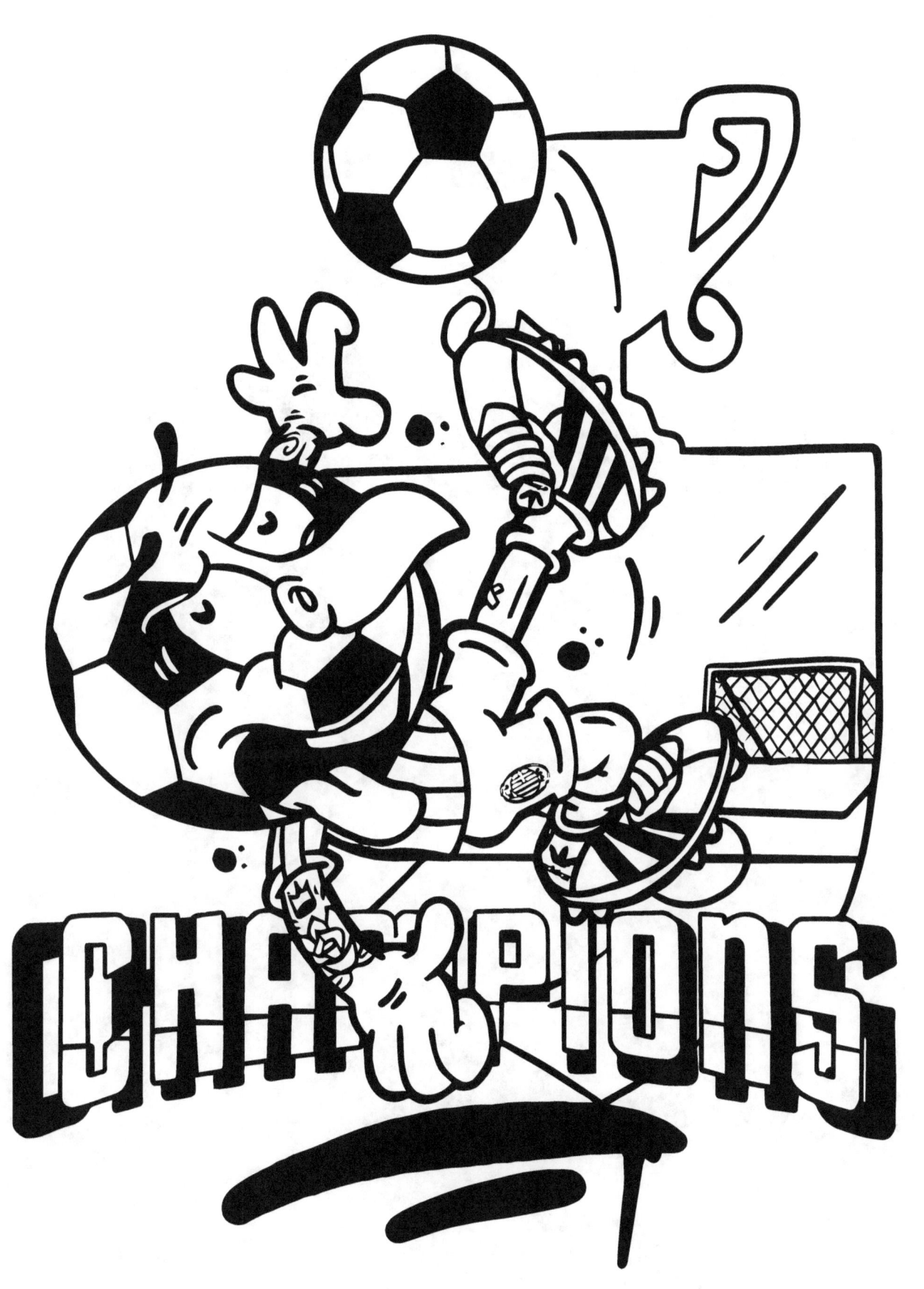

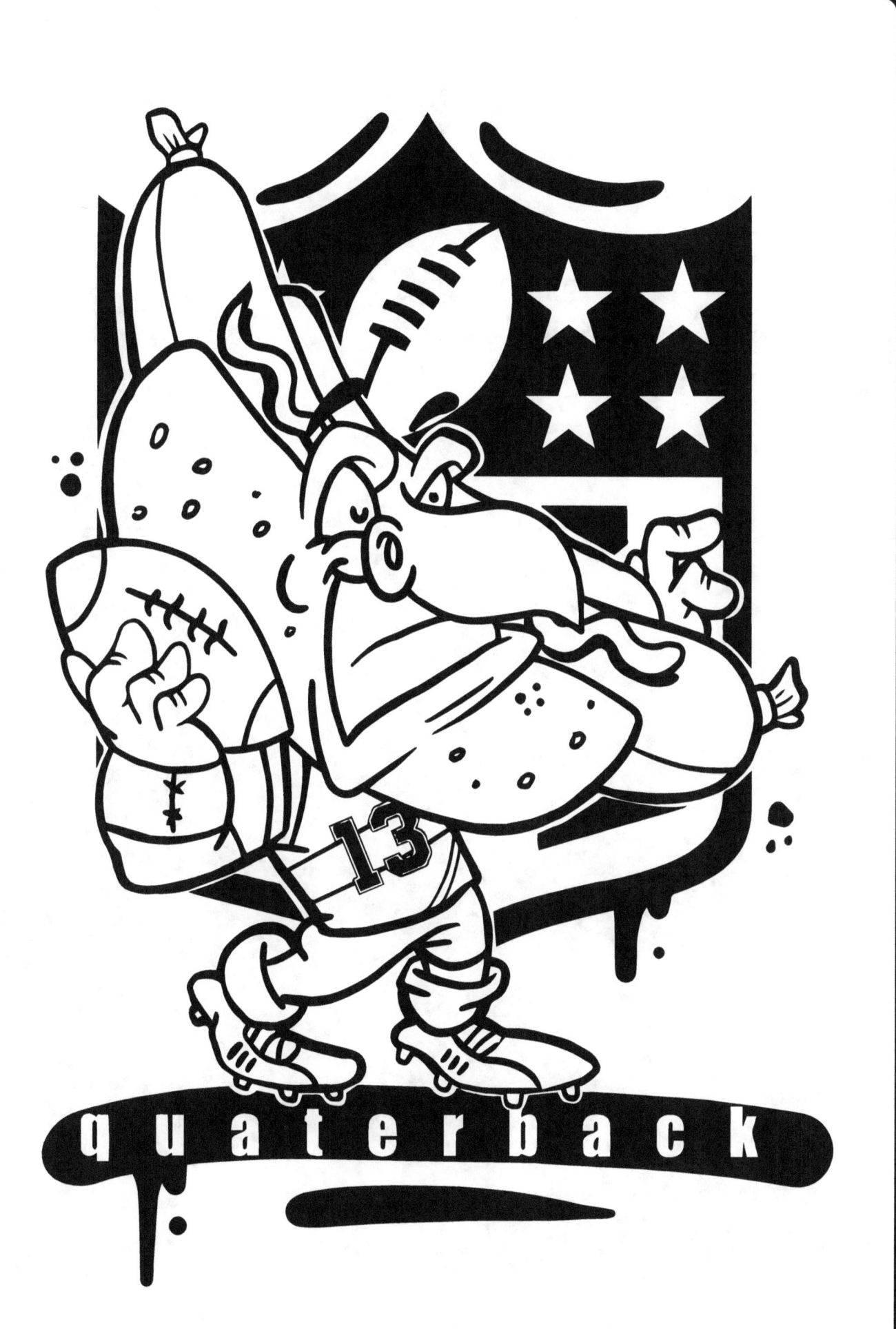

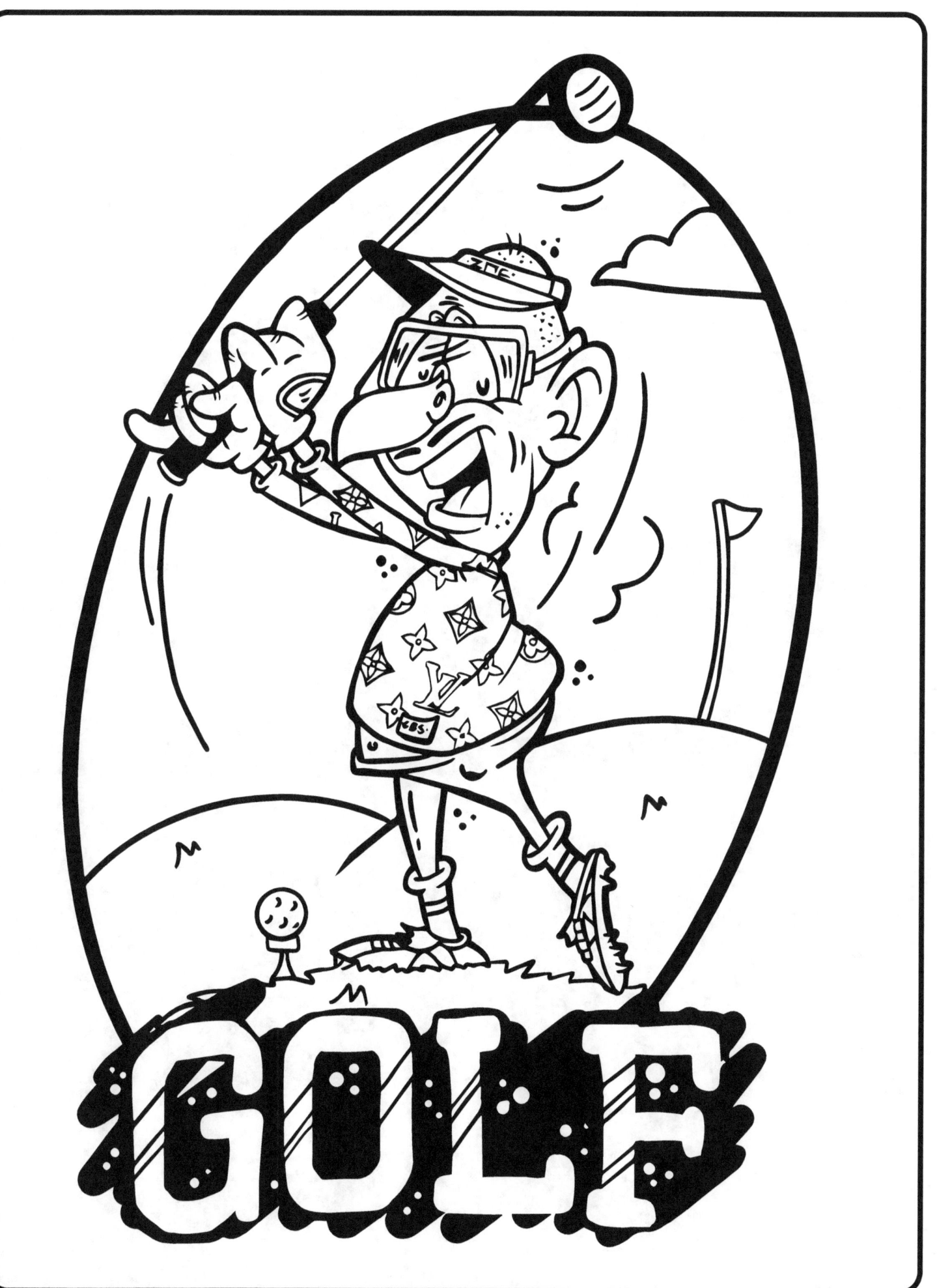

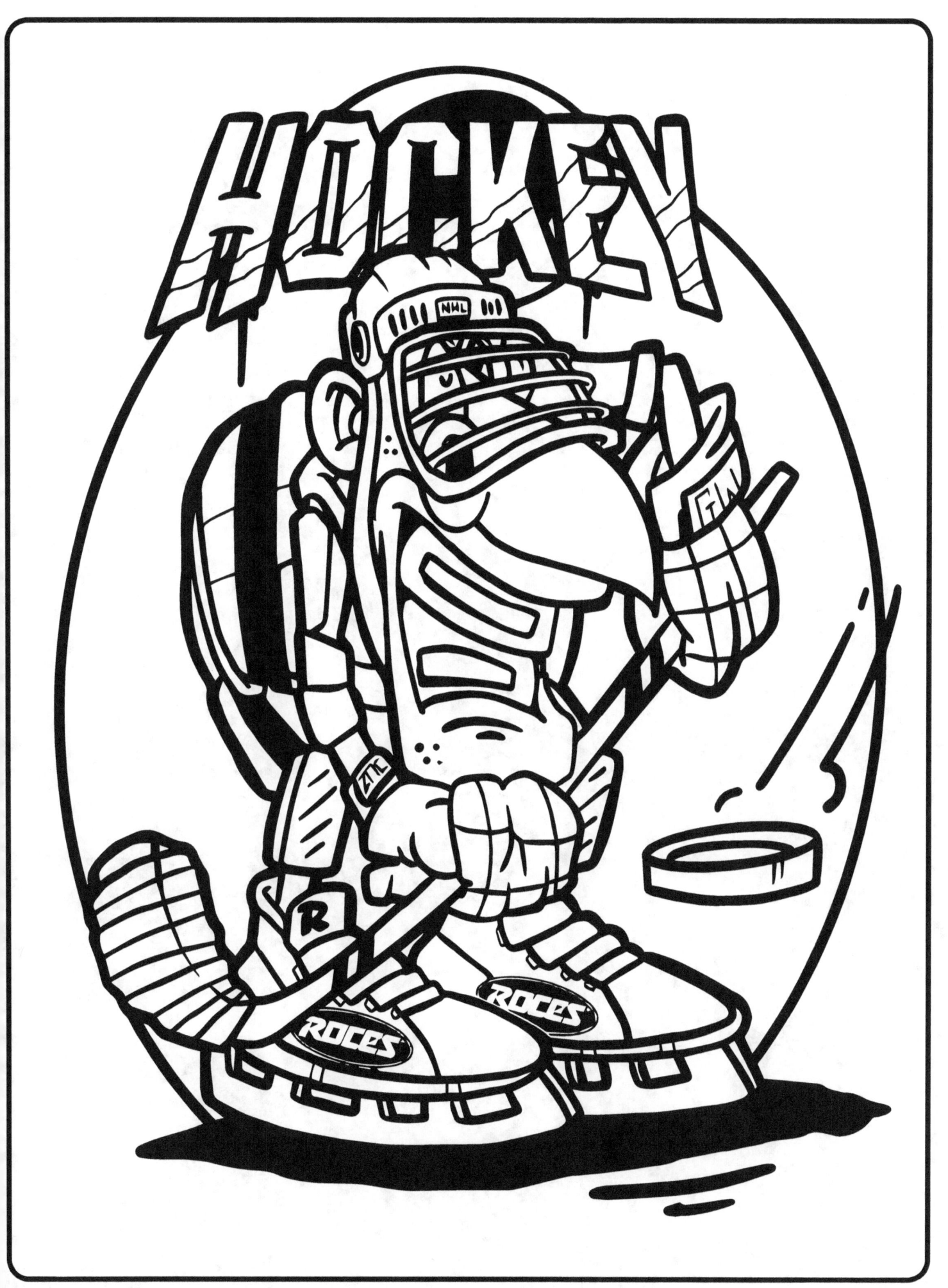

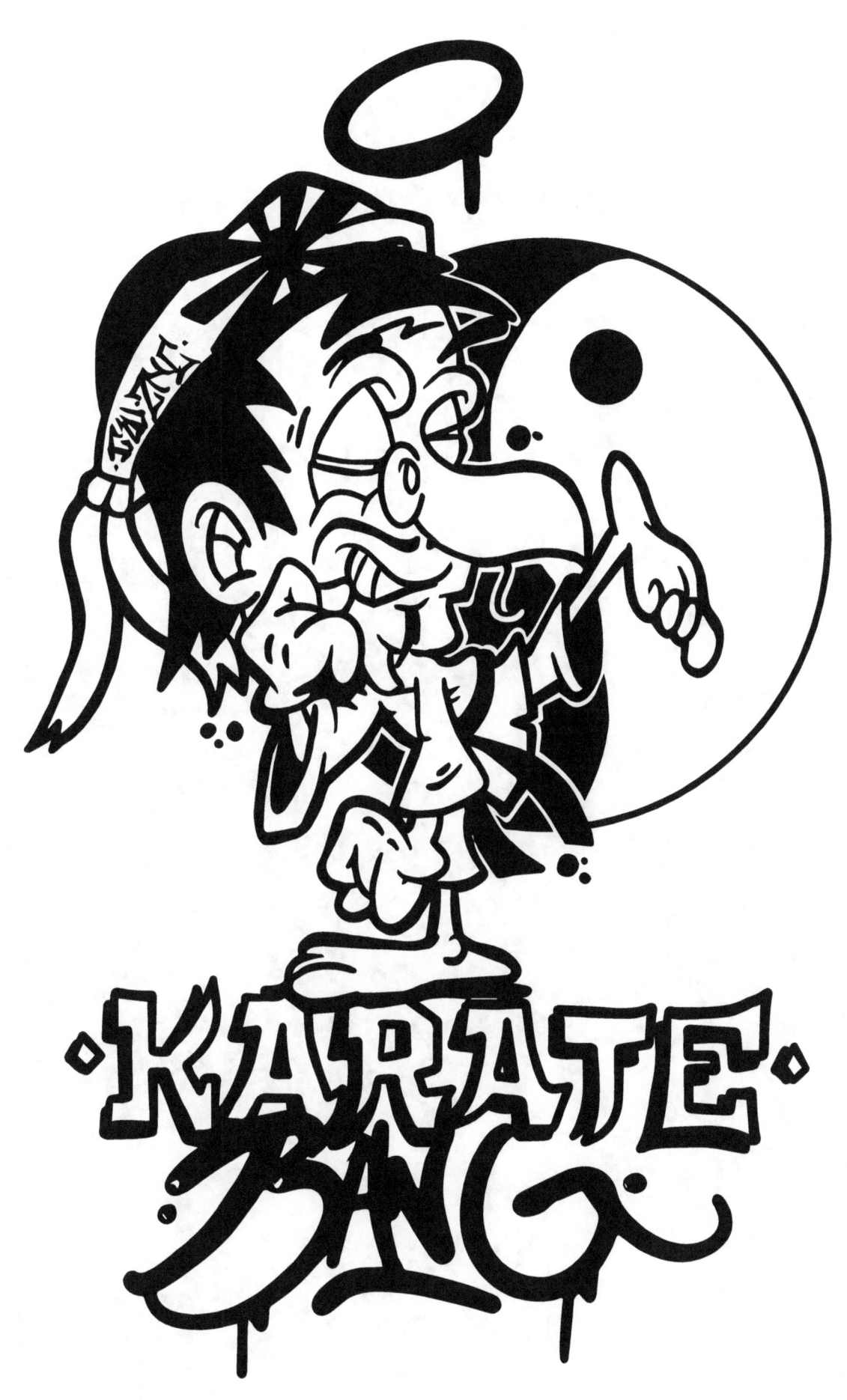

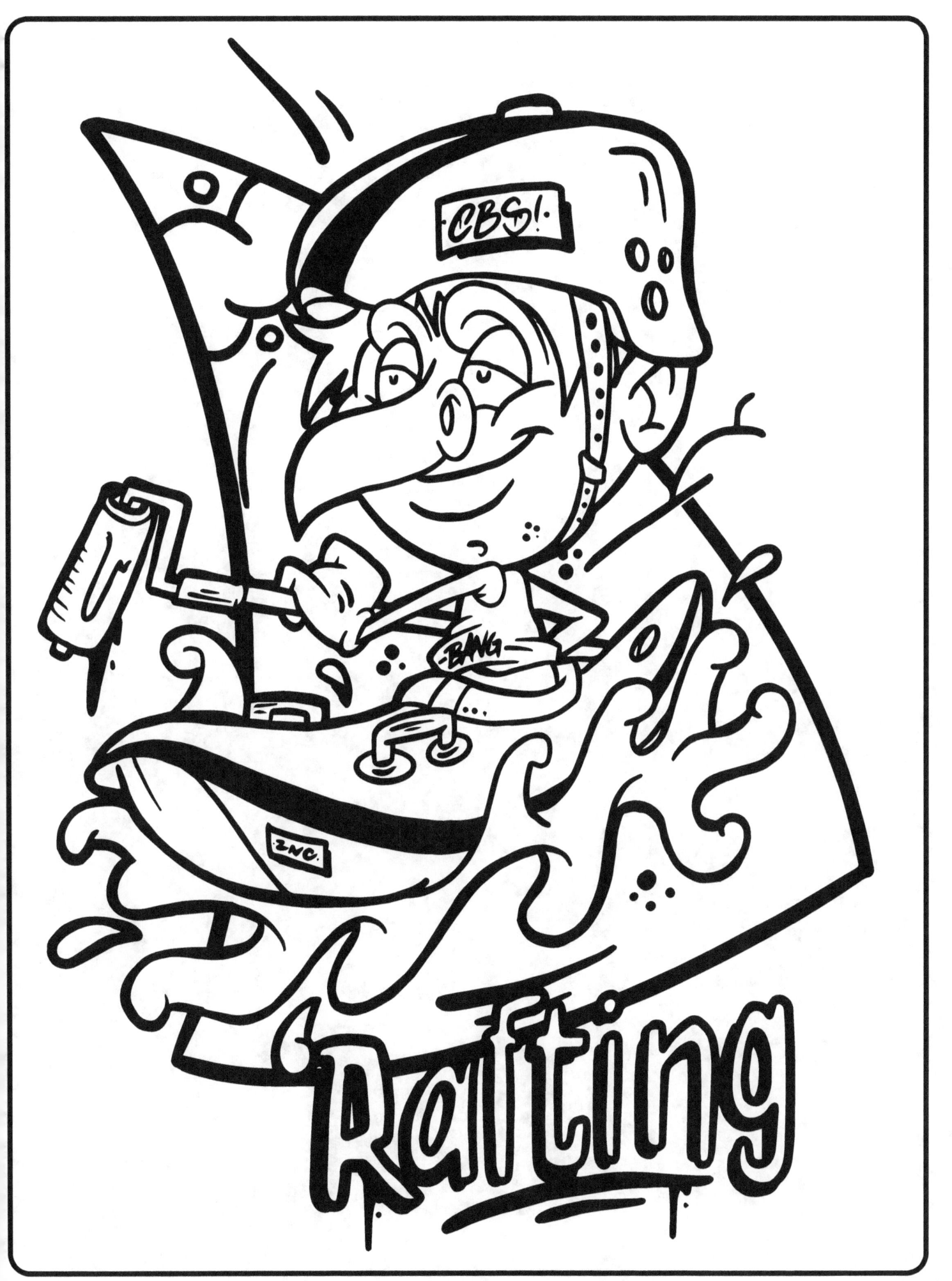

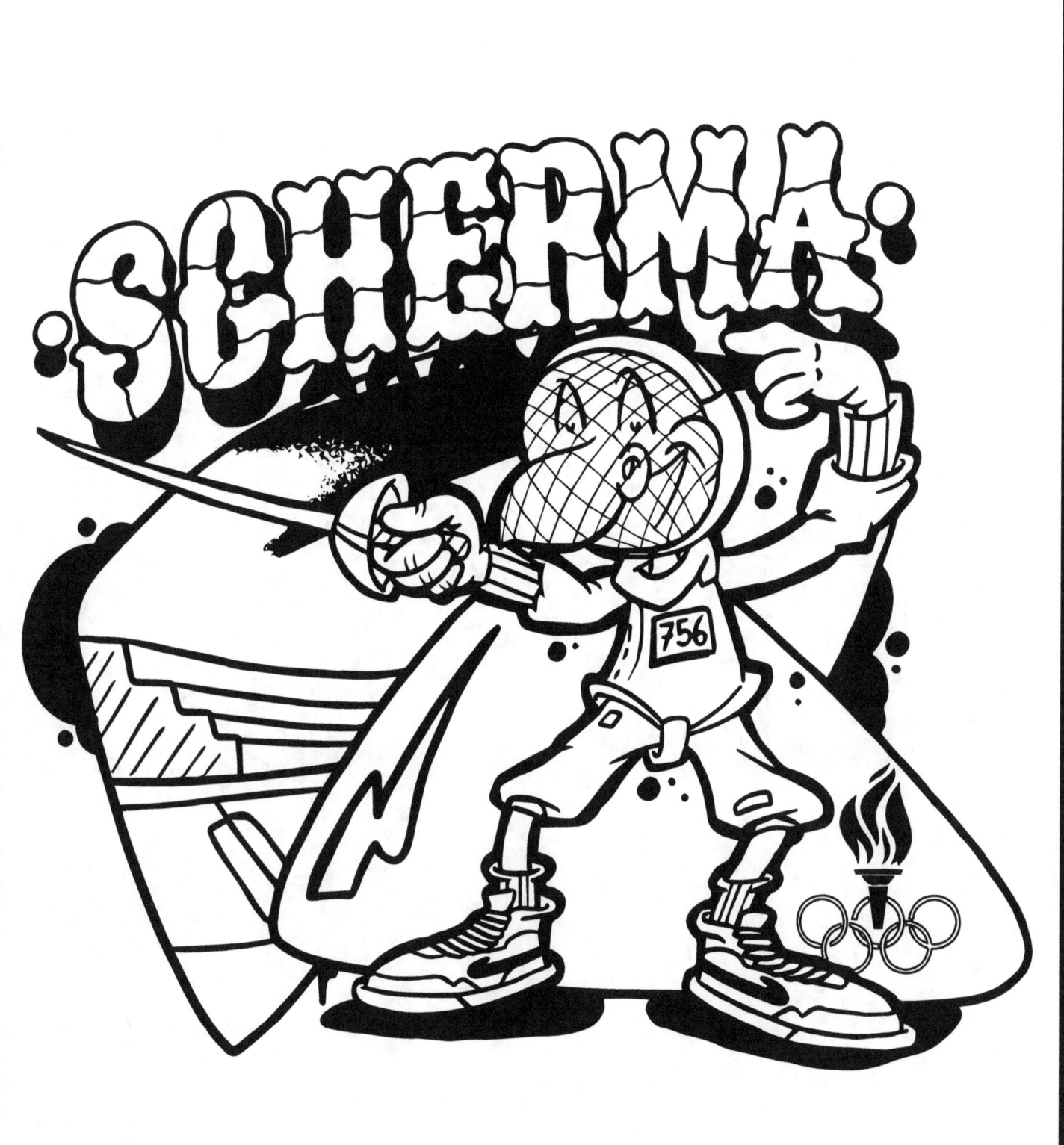

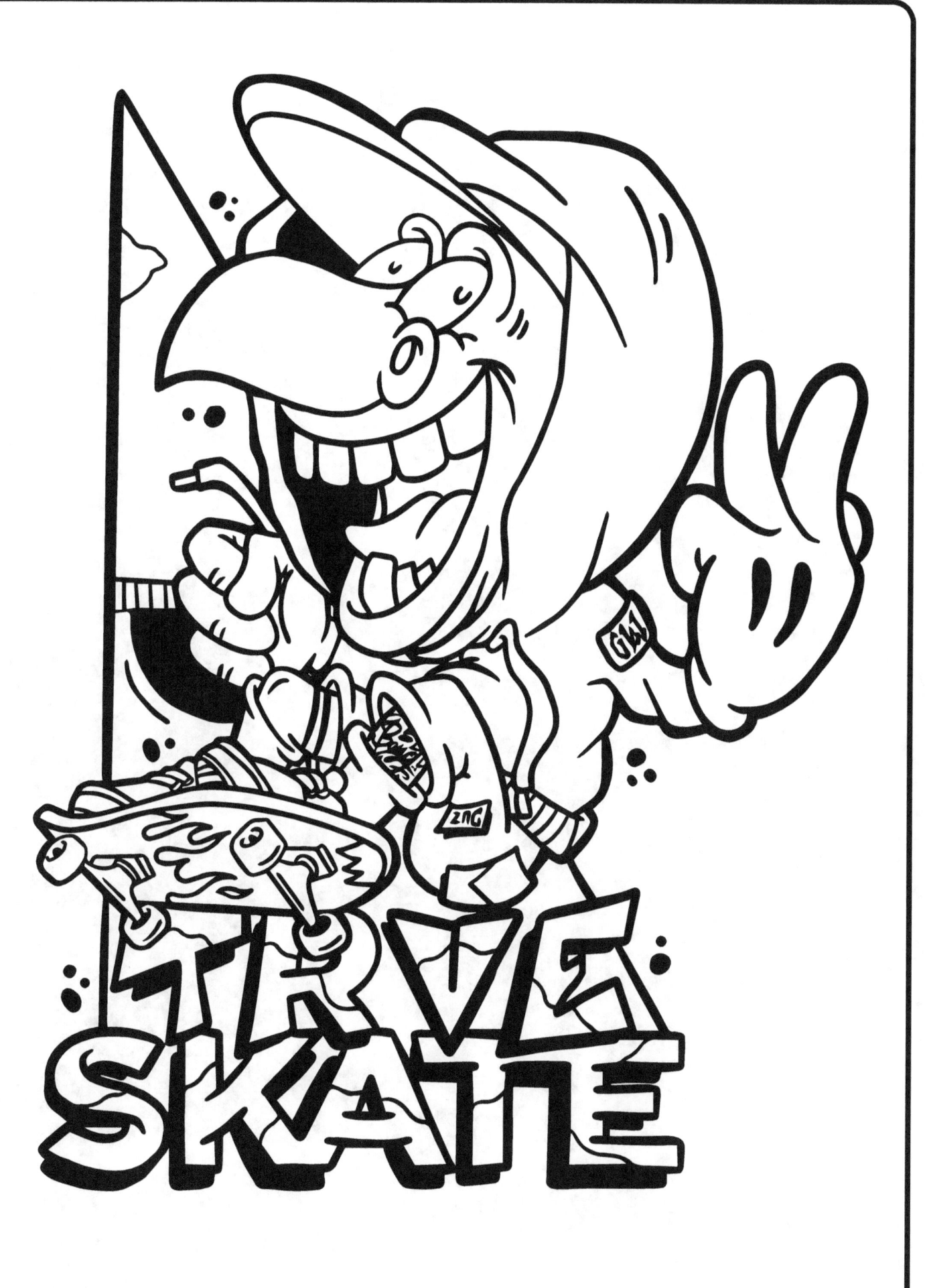

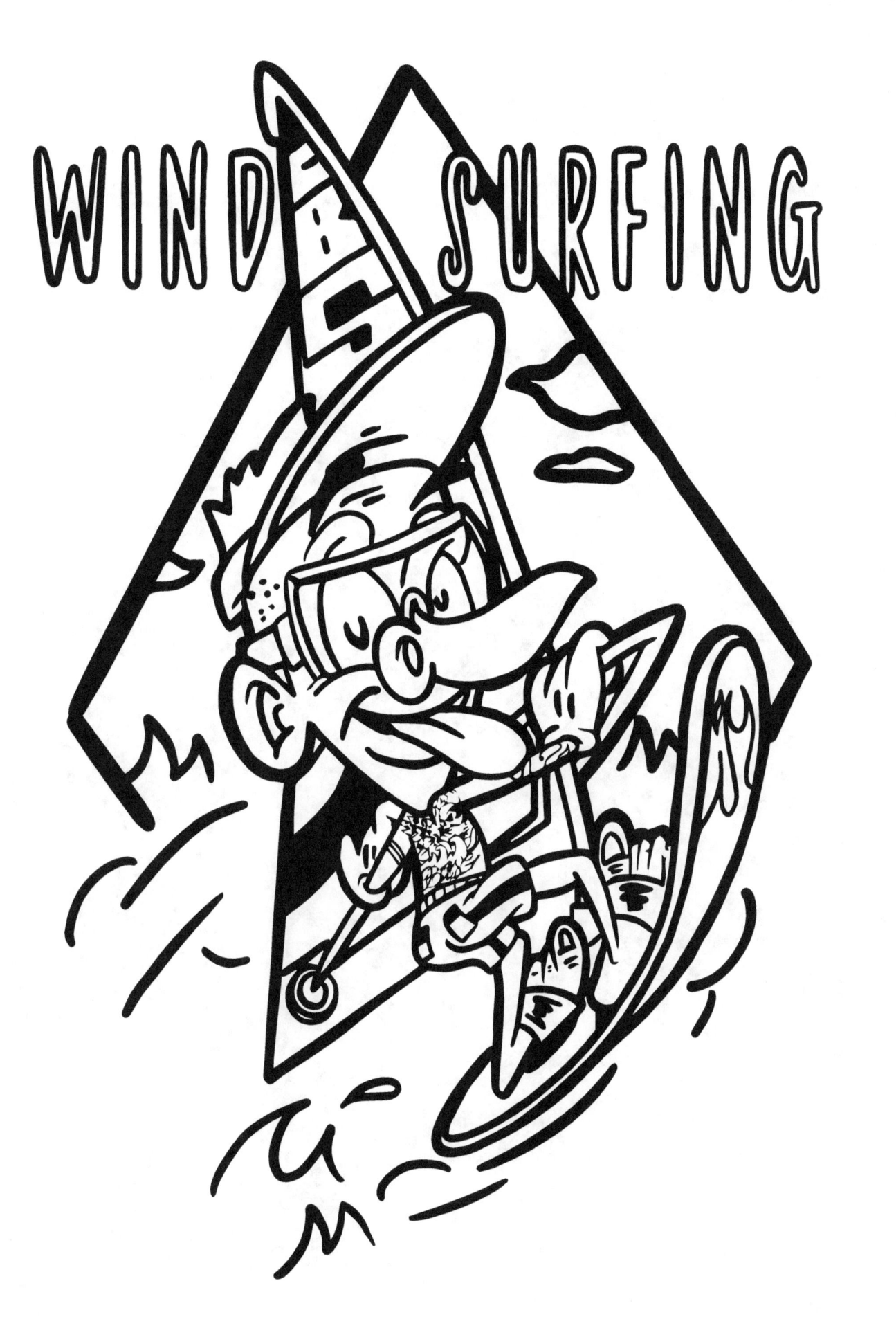

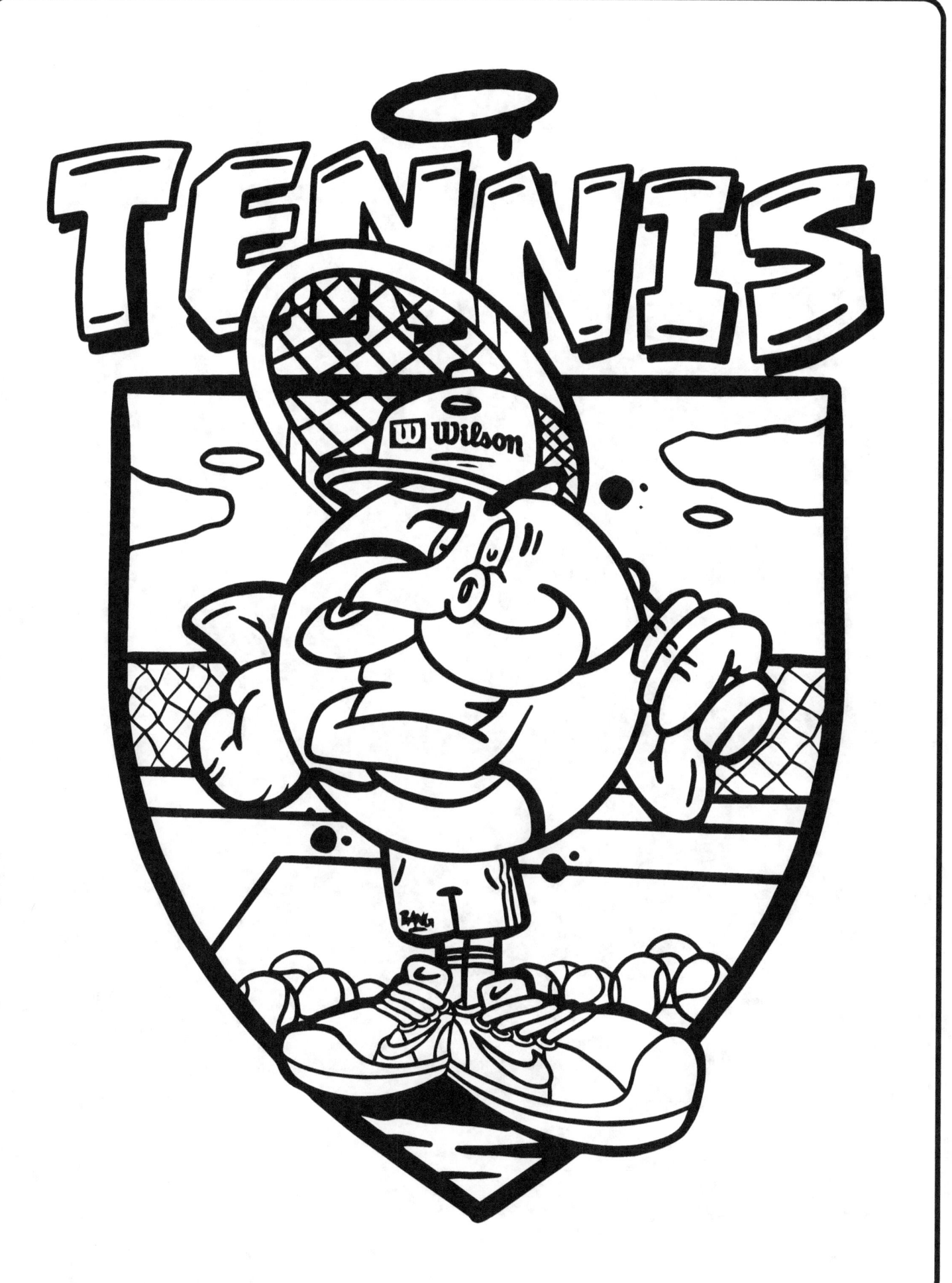

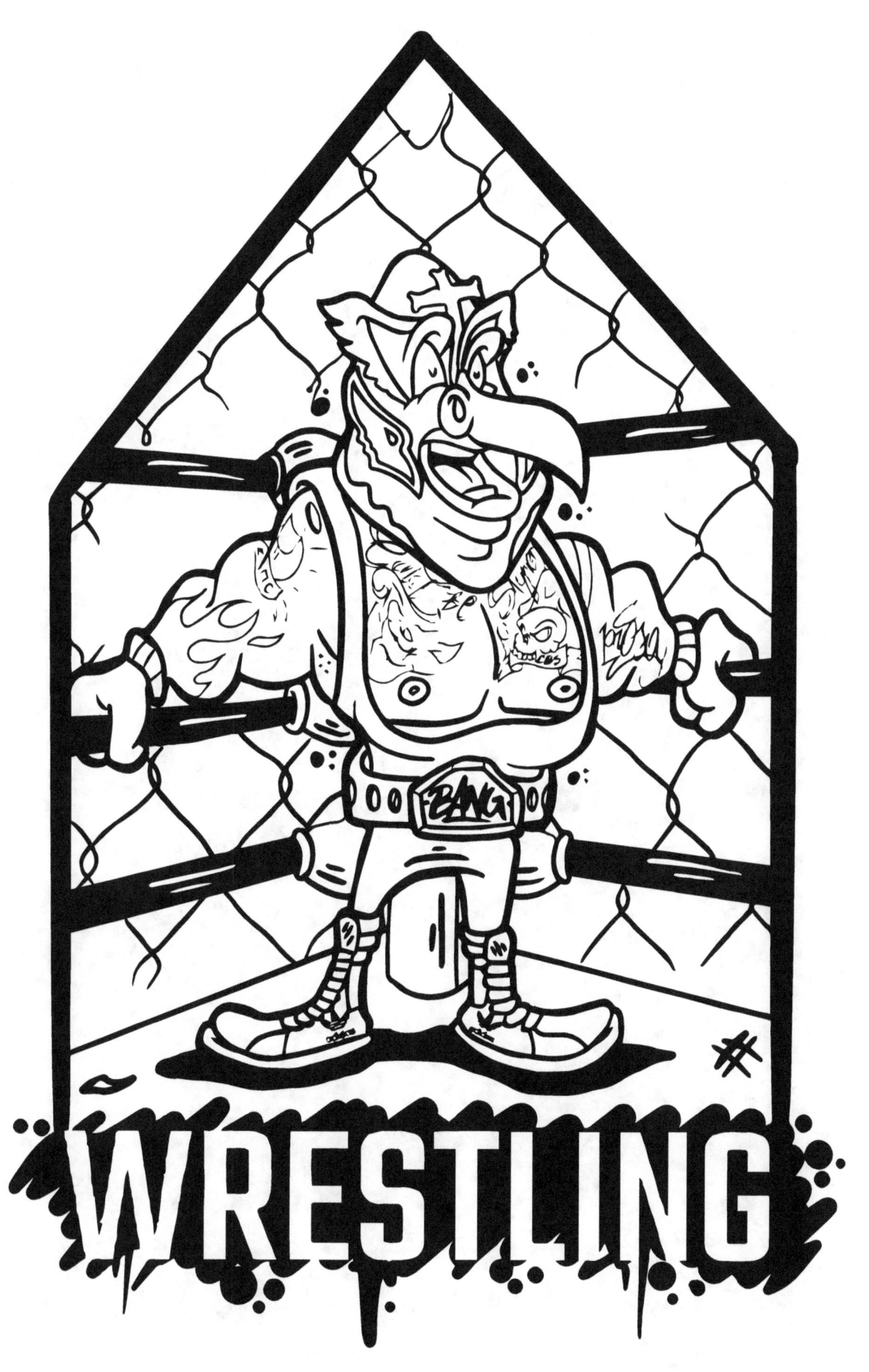

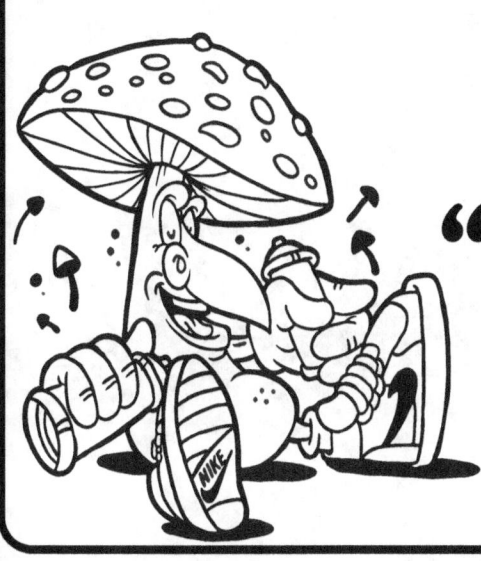

" We are at the end of this colorful adventure, mate! Here's my last task for you: draw your own rendition of Mr. Bang on this page, take a picture of it and send it back to mrbangbooks@gmail.com.
The best one will be featured in the next edition of Graffiti Art Coloring Book.
Take a chanche to win right now! "

For comments, suggestions, ideas for future coloring books or to be updated about next books please send mail to
mrbangbooks@gmail.com
or follow me on Instagram:
@prosa_bang
&
@amazingcoloringbooks

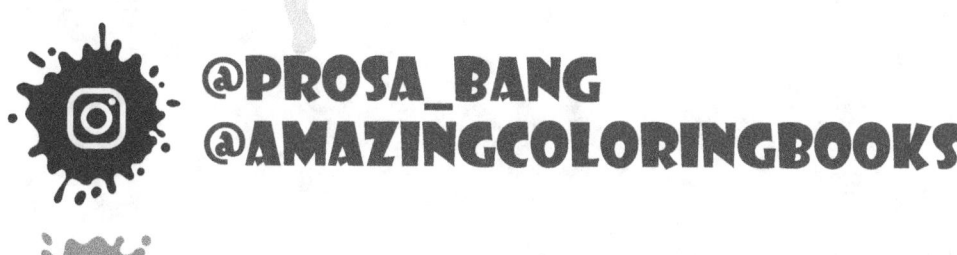
@PROSA_BANG
@AMAZINGCOLORINGBOOKS

MRBANGBOOKS@GMAIL.COM

www.ingramcontent.com/pod-product-compliance
Lightning Source LLC
Chambersburg PA
CBHW081707220526

45466CB00009B/2899